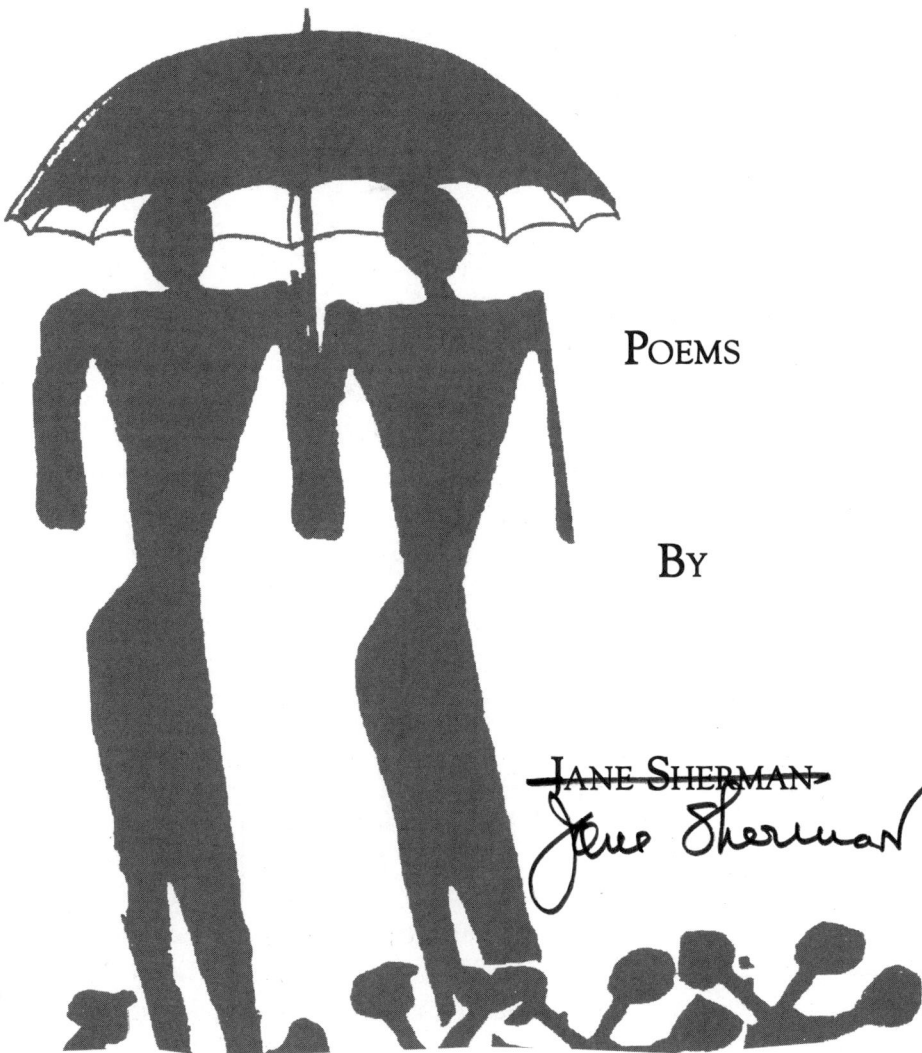

SONGS OF SENESCENCE

POEMS

BY

JANE SHERMAN

Inspired by Fellow Assisted-Living Residents
And

H. Donald Kroitzsh: DESIGNER

Michelle Mathesius: PRODUCER

Pat Catterson: TECHNICAL EDITOR

Ori & Zoe Calman: SECRETARIES

Susan Davison: SPECIAL ASSISTANCE

Five Corners Press: REALIZATIONS

For information or orders contact:
Barbara Davis
The Actors' Fund of America
729 7th Avenue
New York, NY 10019
212-221-7300

JANE SHERMAN
b. Beloit Wisconsin 1908-
m. Ned Lehac 1940-1999

Danced with Ruth St. Denis-Ted Shawn Company on Far East and U.S. tours 1925-1928. Member of original Humphrey-Weidman Company, then appeared in Broadway musicals and as a member of the Radio City Music Hall Rockettes, 1928-1936.

After several years living and studying in Europe, she embarked on a writing career with the publication of five non-fiction juveniles. Then she returned to dance as writer and as the re-creator of St. Denis, Shawn and Humphrey works for the Denishawn Repertory Dancers, which she co-founded, the Martha Graham Company, the Vanaver Caravan, and others for performances in New York City, the Kennedy Center, Jacob's Pillow, the 1990 Biennale de la Danse Américaine, Lyons, France, and elsewhere around the world.

With the the documentary video *Denishawn Dances On!* (Kultur Productions: 2003) she and collaborators, Michelle Mathesius and Livia Vanaver, presented the largest visually-recorded Denishawn repertory in existence.

Jane now resides at the Actors' Fund Assisted-Living Residence in Englewood N.J., where she continues an active creative life.

Books by Jane Sherman

*Soaring: The Diary and Letters of a Denishawn
Dancer in the Far East: 1925-1926*
(pub. 1976)

The Drama of Denishawn Dance
(pub. 1979)

Denishawn: The Enduring Influence
(pub. 1983)

Co-author with Barton Mumaw of his autobiography
Barton Mumaw, Dancer:
From Denishawn to Jacob's Pillow and Beyond
(pub. 1986, repr. 2000)

And her first volume of collected poems
Time is Now
(pub. 1998)

CONTENTS

GIACOSO

For

Michelle

To
The Actors' Fund of America

The Fund is my safety: I shall not want.

Thou maketh me to lie down on soft mattresses:
Thou leadeth me beside the still gardens.

Thou restoreth my health; Thou leadeth me in the
paths of kindliness for your good cause.

Yea, though I walk through hallways in the
shadow of pain, I shall fear no illness; for Thou
art
with me; Thy care and Thy staff, they
comfort me.

Though often Thou preparest a table before me fit
only for mine enemies, Yet Thou blesseth us with
food and drink: My bladder runneth over.

Surely goodness and kindness will follow me the
rest of my life: And I will praise this home Thou
hast provided me forever. Amen!

INTRODUCTIONS

Come meet our actor recounting her glories,
Our diva reliving *Turandot's* high E's.

The Barnum-and-Bailey clown cursing his fate,
The playwright who scowls at his full dinner plate.

Shake hands with the costume man eying our clothes
And the stage manager sneering down sensitive nose.

Greet drama professor behind her thick glasses
Who dreams of the stars she had taught in her classes.

The P.R. guru has no show to promote,
The sideman replays just a single blue note.

The expert in lighting has no spots or gels,
And the doorman hears nothing but curtain-time bells.

Our cameraman's mired in admiring himself.
Our dancer has stored her tutu on the shelf.

The director alone can detect each one's droop
In this miserably madcaply elderly troupe.

THERE COMES A TIME

Leave our trusty eyes afloat
Behind their granny glasses
And our tonsils in our throats
Far from erotic passes.

A fancy walker we don't need
Nor whiter upper denture.
And with our figures gone to seed,
Who wants a cruise adventure?

Our fingernails are pale and blunt,
Hair almost non-existent.
For glowing skin we have to hunt
Between age-spots persistent.

We love our fat — we hate to diet,
All scrawniness is woe.
Alcohol incites to riot —
But whatta way to go!

PILGRIMAGE

Daily after breaking fast
the residential sisters and greyed monks
plod each toward solitary cell
to seek, with power of belief,
their quintessential relief.

VITALS

Once a month they sound our parts
To discover how we thrive,
And from these numbers on our charts
They decide who's still alive.

FIRST BITE OF THE APPLE

The optimist sees the hole but not the worm.
The pessimist sees the worm but not the flesh.
The realist sees half a worm.
The opportunist only sees pie.

TO MY TABLE-MATE

Oh, do stop whining while we're dining,
Inflicting me with loud tirades!
Your whimpering falls on my deaf ears:
Last night I lost my hearing aids.

A Patient To Her Doctor: Morning Rounds

My doctor who art approaching
Familiar be thy name.
Thy comfort come, thy will be done
At home as it is in hospital.
Give me this day my daily pill
And forgive me my complaining
As I forgive those who complain around me.
Lead me not into hypochondria
But deliver me from pain—
For thine is the knowledge, the power, and the science
To save me forever (I hope!)

NOT NECESSARILY

Adam thought that Eve was sweet,
All innocence defined.
He bit the apple, looked again,
And promptly changed his mind.

Cain, a man whom no one liked,
Was often very violent.
He struck his brother Abel down,
Thus rendering him dead silent.

Bathsheba, spied on in her bath,
Was one unhappy lady.
No makeup on, her hair uncurled,
She screamed, "I am not ready!"

Gabriel blows a hotter horn
Than Satchmo, it is said,
For Satch can only raise the roof
While Gabe can raise the dead.

Trusting Noah, two by two,
Those rescued in his Ark
Were glad to reach the Promised Land
But found no place to park.

Salome was a real spoiled brat,
A beauty and a baddy.
She demanded poor John's head
Before she'd dance for daddy.

TAKE IT FROM A TOUGH OLD BIRD

It hurts to get hit in your perfect poise,
It pains to get punched in your vanity.
It aches to acknowledge you're playing with toys
In this elderly game of inanity.

It's a curse to see men turn away from you
When you've always been Belle of the Ball.
But it's worse when they beg to come stay with you
Then replay the foreplay — that's all.

My knees have retired, my décollétage sags.
My skull shows through gaps in my hair.
My eyes are enpouched into old travelling bags
And wherever I'm going, I've been there.

Yet this leathery hen will not call it a day
Nor has any intention to do so,
For my wattles are up and I'm on my way
To as many farewells as Caruso.

TO OUR CHEF:

When you're out of tater tots — it's pasta
When your turkey has the trots — it's pasta
When your inspiration's slow
And your budget's running low
And your mind's about to blow — it's pasta!

    Vermicelli, rigatoni,
    Tagliatelle, macaroni,
    Penne, bow knots, tortellini,
    Angel hair and spagettini —
    One more plate of manicotti,
    We'll inflate like Pavarotti!!

To prevent this dire disasta
No more with the starch of pasta —

        BASTA!!!

THE FLIRT

What image from a dream-dazed mind
Propels bold flaunt before male eyes
Of hem at heels beneath your robe
To signal summit's lush surprise?

What charms had midnight fantasy wrought
To lure above glimpsed nightgown edge
One so adept at climbing flanks
He'd yearn to mount *your* barren sedge?

Why do we care? Why greedy stare
If your enticement should succeed?
Could bare desire have so exposed
The secret of our private need?

GENETICS

You cannot will a poem
Nor clone a perfect life
Nor fabricate a butterfly
From stolid, gray-moth wife.

You cannot forbid grief
Nor shape the pain it brings,
Nor from a sparrow's throat
Lure song the skylark sings.

EXPERIENCE SPEAKS

Oh, a wig's a fine and private thing
When your skull grows bare and old.
It keeps your brains from shivering
In exposure to the cold.
But when the summer days flare hot,
It's not.

AU COURANT

The corset, once *de rigeur* wear
For every lady here and there,
Was banished into chic thin air
Until revived with *un vrai flair*
To live anew *sur derrière*
As bawdy, brazen *bustière*.

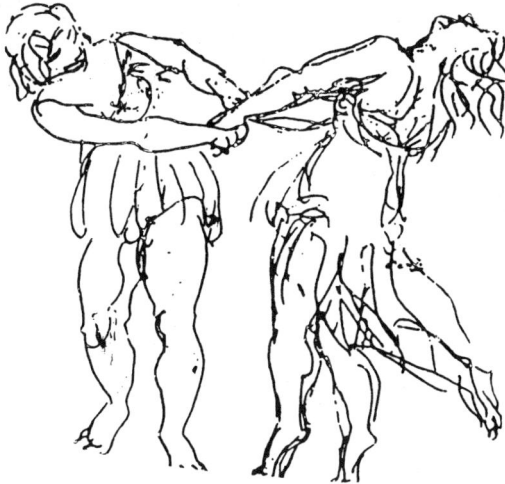

TEMPTATIONS

Come dance with me in coltish glee
Upon the luscious grasses hence
Where we can prance lasciviously,
Escaped from barbed-wired, no-sin fence!

POEM FOR PAUL

At my table bright this morn
Stopped a gentle leprechaun.
"How be ye, M'am?" quoth he, quirky.
"Why, I be fine, sir," says I, perky.

"May I ask you," then spoke he,
"To write a poem just for me?"
I was stunned with flustered pride
(Although I hid it well inside).
I blushed to red and hung my head
And with great effort, "Yes," I said.

He grinned a grin from ear to ear
And left me lone in frightful fear
To struggle out with pen and wit
A verse for him — and this is it.

SONG FOR A SMOGGY DAY

As a child did you not jump
Up behind the horse's rump
To perch on Grandpa's driving seat
High above her trotting feet?

On such a sweet and muggy day
The buggy smelled of sweat and hay,
Of clover and old harness leather
Mixed deliciously together.

And when the mare her trumpet blew,
Releasing golden dung for you,
Your giggles floated to the sky
As Naughty! Free! You blew reply.

FEMINIST

[To the melody "Everything's up-to-date in Kansas City" from *Oklahoma!*]

I threw away my bra when Gloria Steinem
Said we should not wear 'em anymore
My lipstick I withdrew
And my mascara, too,
As I prepared to fight the sexist war.

My 4-B cup too quickly did expand out
Into the forty-D I never wore
I did everything
To make our leader sing
And soon my bosoms almost reached the floor.

I let my hair grow back its natural color
And never shaved my legs from toes to top
I haven't bought high heels
Or eaten fatty meals
Or had some juicy feels since I joined up.

So goodbye to the hopes and dreams and battles
To resignation and despair "Hello"
I am in distress
Because my life's a mess
And I've gone about as far as I can go
Yes! I've gone about as far as I can go!

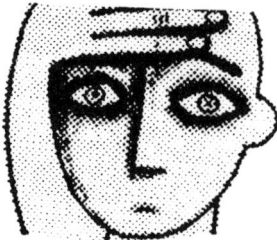

WARNING: AGING MAY BE HAZARDOUS TO YOUR HEALTH

Watch out for moments when you cannot tell
Your one and only left hand from your right
And will not know what day it is, or year,
Nor if the time be dawn or darkest night.

One evening, coughing strongly at a party,
You'll learn why pale slacks are a big mistake,
And that while laughing at the festive table
You may eject your plate upon your plate.

Be careful! Don't take steps into the void
For they could land you on your derrière
With fractured coccyx and a bruised libido
Unlike those early days far merrier.

But if despair becomes the only answer
To frailties that make you shake and sway,
Remember one prescription that will help you:
Call up your local deity – and pray!

THE HERMIT

Don't take me out to the ballgame,
Don't lure me into the park.
Don't drive me around to see foliage
Until it is supper-time and almost dark.
For I don't understand ballgames
And what can we do in the park?
But it's "One! Two! Three! And you're out!"
If you don't take part.

Don't call me down to play bingo,
Nor urge me in to play pool.
I'd much rather read in my lovely room
Than follow the laws of the Golden Rule.
For I don't want to be herded
Like a sheep being sent to the fair –
So next time it's "Three!" and I'm out
'Cause I won't be there.

INVARIABLY

Into your eyes the grapefruit spurts
And grape juice falls on clean, starched shirts,
But orange juice has no preferance
For jackets, vests, or tailored pants.

Blueberries like to spread their gore
Over teeth and tongue and more,
Altho raspberries seem inclined
To shed their blood on skirts, I find.

Tomatoes aim below the belt
Of Christian, Muslim, Jew, or Celt.
And beet juice wages a nuclear war
On every damned necktie I wore.

Hot tea maintains the meanest hold
On all it stains, from tan to gold,
While coffee dribbles without fail
From avid mouth to craven tail.

So after learning in the Navy
That all—whites seduce all gravy,
I now dress to make me glad
And, as the canny Scots, wear plaid.

THE GAME

**There is a game two actors play
after their dinner every day:**

"Who was she, Pat, with that satin skin
and blue eyes so deep you could dive right in?"
"Yes! Yes! She was gorgeous. I see her now!
Remember the way she could milk a bow?"
"Of course I do. But what was her *name*?
And what was the play where she earned so much fame?
She was fantastic, the audience was great.
On opening night they – what was that damned date?"
"Who cares anymore? Remember her *Hedda*?"
"Oh, what a voice! She could have sung *Nedda*."
"Her leading man was – it's just on my tongue –
Was it Morley? Or Mason? Or that idiot Young?"
"None of them, Johnny, but who was it – Who?"
"Well it sure wasn't me, and it sure wasn't you!"
"Pat, why do we now lose their names from our minds
when once we could memorize hundreds of lines?"
"I don't know, Johnny. It doesn't seem right."
"No. It isn't – oh, well – Good night."

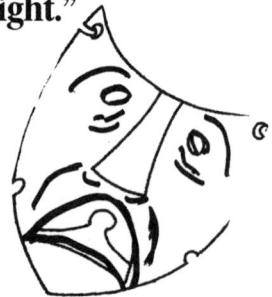

A RESIDENT SALUTES IRVING BERLIN

Oh how I hate to go down to our dinner
Oh how I dread what I may be fed
Rubb'ry veal and collard greens
Pasta, rice, and black-eyed beans

My belly will growl!
My breath will be foul!
My face will be blue in the morning!

Some day I'm going to torture the cook-staff
To make them holler and weep and wail
And then I'll get that other pup
The one who writes our menus up
And eat what's left of my life in jail!

CHORUS SONG

Come praise the ubiquitous carrot,
Its shape and its color and smell,
And the hundreds of ways it is served us —
Then banish the damned thing to hell!

DINING CHEZ NOUS

From intellectual corner of the room
opinionated voices soar, to boom
their views of opera and *le Cinéma Noir*,
boasting of the stars they knew or are.

Across the way plebians demonstrate
a pitcher's glorious throws, strike-outs and fate,
replaying games lost long ago, like fools,
as steaming soup at first base stops and cools.

Between, ignoring clash of egos, sit
our subtle snobs in customary snit
of scorn for *bulvan* and élite alike,
enjoying arcane irony in quiet.

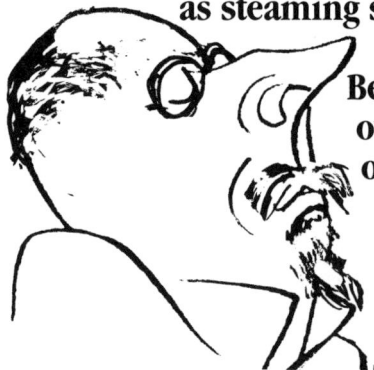

One Mo' Time

Darling, will you kiss me once,
Then kiss me once again?
It's been a long, long time –

There's no reason to resist
Such perfect bliss as this.
You know it's not a crime –

Altho' I never was a star attraction
My white hair is now a sad distraction –

So close your eyes and kiss me once
And maybe even more –
We haven't got much time.

The Eavesdropper

Behind me, charming, they at table sit
Exchanging memories across the years.
Chicago formed his actor skill and wit:
Kentucky shaped her teacher pioneers.

With jokes and family recipes, they flirt
In back-and-forth too polished to be crude.
No topic lasts from bouillon to dessert;
No sadness is permitted to intrude.

Their tales are not Vienna's woodsy dream
But home-songs from the cradle overheard
Of pleasures pumpkin-plain so rich with cream
That I compelled to memorize each word.

ADVICE FROM A SOCIAL WORKER

"Ladies, when you're eighty-two
You must be careful what you do.

"Hands must show no spots or tarnish.
Nails must glow with coats of varnish.
Diet! No more sweets for you.
Dye your hair bewitching blue.
Guard bare skin from taint of tan.
Girdle tight your spreading can.

"Drink your milk (osteoporosis).
Exercise to cure neurosis.
Gargle against halitosis.
Outrun diverticulosis!"

"But, Miss," I interrupt to ask,
"If we must do such daily task
Who'd ever want to live to be
This masquerading eighty-three?
                    Not me!"

IN THE LOST LATITUDES

The grave is not the only place
Where, methinks, but few embrace,
For here desire's a feeble thing
That seldom achieves love-making.

[Unless a serendipitous flame
Ignites libidinous male and dame.]

THE MERRY WIDOW

I have no teeth, I wear a wig.
I can no longer dance a jig.
My temper's foul, my outlook poor.
Tall handsome boors have lost allure.
I hear no more as keen as bat.
I often wonder where I'm at.
I've lost my guidepost — husband, son,
And every lover, one by one.
Yet...
Would witted widower want a wife,
Could I amuse him thro' new life?

I think I could! I think I could!

Poco Lento

For

Ned

WAITING FOR THE SNOW

Tire chains hang on garage walls above paired listless boots
And bags of salt lounge at a shovel's foot.

On kitchen marble-top a roast defrosts.

Upstairs bright parkas, mittens, ear-muffs, scarves
Blossom like flowers through the quiet nursery,
And the old one looks from wheelchair
Out to glooming sky.

She pulls a blanket tight against the words
"Falling softly — Softly falling — "
Tick-tocking through her head.
"Snow falling faintly on the Universe..."
Yes, she said.
"Faintly falling on all the living and the dead."
Oh, yes! she said.

Waiting......

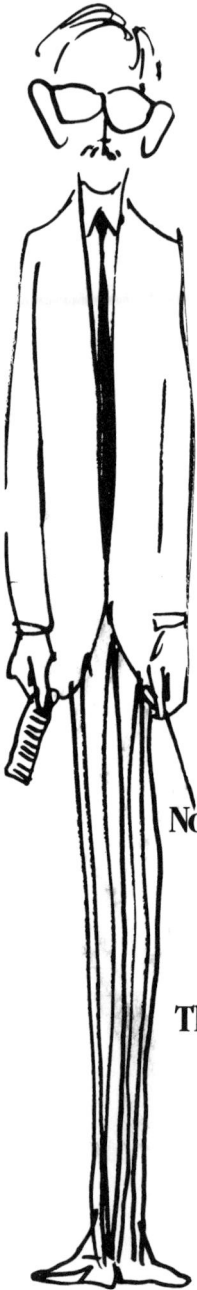

THE STAGE MANAGER

Now is the hour of the rabbit and the bedding bird,
of whispering river and the homeless wind,
when bullfrog from the pit sounds glottal A
alerting cricket-strings to tune
the usher-fireflies away.
Then as Orion climbs from dimmer to full bright,
you signal cue for curtain-rise
upon the drama of our night.

INDEPENDENCE DAY

I pledge no allegiance to God or to king
Nor nation nor flag – but this one thing:
To truth incorruptible on battered throne,
Rejected, uncouth, relentless – alone.

TO THE POET GERALD STERN

"Fall in love at ninety-one?
Bah!" the savants bray,
Voices reverberating down
From Galileo's day.

But I could teach them something that
Such asses never learn:
One touch of stranger's poetry
Can set old wood a-burn.

DISOVERING NEW WORDS

Croodle me in your arms
And poosk my weary head
For I am quanked —
And fearful of a world where vermin crawl
In politics and pew.

IN HUBBLE'S EYE

It does not matter
if the plains erupt in boils tomorrow,
and fields of waving oats —
all bedded flesh — and stalking cats turn ash.
Nor, when sequoias shrivel
and oceans gulp their truant sands
and our somersaulting planet stumbles
over Pleiades and meteors
in race from galaxy to galaxy,
will it matter one scorching tinker's damn —
except to me.

MUST

Must you so desperately be gone,
Your manzanilla curdled, corked, and wan,
Your cornered scent as cold as graveyard rust,
Your footsteps blotted in the roadway dust?

Our bed retains no stigma of embrace.
Our mirror reflects no gargoyle of your face.
Our walls no more reverberate with lust
Than with guitar's wry whisper through dry must.

And when no shadow smirks beside the fire,
Must I so desperately desire?

COCKTAIL HOUR

I breathe the lilac air enfumed
with pesticides from false-green lawns,
and face the tarnished sun.
I dare not cup a single drop
from gangreened brook that once ran thro' the watercress
and mossed the seal-head stones.

Nor dare I wipe away one tear
lest I too clearly see
how civilized we be.

TOO LATE

I was never taught the lesson of demand
When young and fresh and bold,
And who, since I have learned it, heeds –
Now I am ugly, frail, and old?

MAY

Now lures the luminescent hour of day
When children find erotic hint of play
And adolescents generate first bliss
In struggle of sweet clumsiness to kiss.
The mothers with each other sit and chat
Of scars and lovers, styles, and this and that,
Their voices monotone as willow-ware
With wedding pattern crackled and worn bare.
The elders' light converse disguises fear
Of solitary night fast moving near
On red-faced clouds that fade into a sleep
Where widows soft retire alone to weep.
And so begins and so completes again
The cycle of spring's fresh, green, learning pain.

MISS MARY ON THE VELDT

Papa, I have crammed your space
With white hunters, books, and other bores,
To leave no corner where a fangéd tiger lurks
In vengeance for safaris never taken
And those that, unforgiven, were —
Why was your space so full
Yet mine now rimless void?

PAPA CALLS FROM KETCHUM

Your space is what you make it, daughter,
And mine was carved in granite prose
Of Spain and fishing streams and bullring lore
And shrapnel shards of war.
This is the hard labor each must do,
So be beginning — be beginning —
Now that I am through.

DEMENTIA AMERICANA: VIETNAM
(The nightmare of our youth)

I live in the town of Womb
In the State of Catatonia
Midway between Alienation
And the Grave.

Each night my sun flames
Napalm clouds
And every dawn my moon lights
Silver bamboo ashes.

My flowers lift their rainbow heads
From roots plunged planet-deep to blood
And no rice grows between my lettuce
Rows on rows.

My Brahms blares tympani of mortars,
Brazens brass of jets, and keens the violins of bombs
Descending
Through my solitary padded cell.

No one hears my panic scream.

CLAVELITOS*

Come ruffling raggedy skirts
Above your long green legs,
My sweet and saucy ones!
Tell me what the years have stolen.

Remind me how the smoke of candle-flesh
Lifts from prayers into the arched and granite dark,
And how dwarf orange trees in their tubs
Perfume Giralda's feet.
Talk of *olés* bellowing from bullring throat
Across the river to Triana's ear,
And of geranium graffiti on white barrio walls
Where water falls like petals.

But float no whisper on your cinnamon breath
Of that mad midnight in moon-drunk death
When he and I saw Miuras dancing on the ice-blue grass –
Lest I remember more that came to pass.

*   Note on *Clavelitos* (Carnations)
     This is a memory of Sevilla, with world's largest Gothic cathedral:
     Giralda is its Moorish tower.
     Triana its gypsy area.
     Miuras are famous fighting bulls.

A MOTHER ASKS
(An actor-resident remembers)

What did they do to you, my son,
My first, my brave, my smiling one,
My boy-child growing to manhood, strong,
Muscled with courage, doing no wrong?
Why thrust the white arm through the night
To choke off your vision of the light?
And when did you know, before you died,
That those who promised life had lied?

Your father cut down the pear tree to mourn
The day he had planted it, when you were born.
But how did I bear the coming Spring
Without hope of its blossoming?

EGO WHINE

If you make mock of my attempts
    (as well you might)
Submerge your smile, I beg, below your hand.
For I am old and vulnerable
And do not understand
The wittery rewarded through the land.

My jingles may not merit praise, God wot,
But with creators everywhere, I plot
To give to form a meaning — to meaning form —
A goal so rarely reached that I will not.
Thus be so kind as never to reveal
The full contempt for me I know you feel.

WHERE AWAY?

The wheelchair push is heavy
with abandoned weight.
Your innocent, sea-gray eyes search
forward through a mist,
as from the hearing-shell curled 'round your ear
whine distant seagull cries.

Entrusted to my steering hands
your barren pate,
your child-like, silken nape,
lure fingers to forgotten touch.

I miss you.

LONG DAY'S JOURNEY

I walk the pot of soup
along wall handrail
from pantry to the jail cell of your pain,
and fill your sweet, resisting mouth
with cautious spoonfuls
before I walk it back again.

WHEN

I will not put on widow's weeds
to veil my face from view.
Nor bind my head with vines of guilt
nor laden my heart with rue.
I will not burden comforters
with my weight of fears.
Nor lacerate my grief
with salted whip of tears.
I will not tolerate self-pity
as soothing balm for woe.
Nor advertise my solitude
to passing friend or foe.

How certain my defiance rings
Even as I do these things ——

AMATEUR

Years of you had not prepared me for goodbye,
nor any parent, poet, friend or book or mentor
marked map for me to follow
thro' this stunned stupidity
where guilt presumes to teach me how to cry.

WIDOW-SPEAK

You dare not ghost to snapshots
and a pair of salt-stained jeans
until my fingertips erase your sea-drugged stare
and I have polished with my grief
one uncharred bone from your fine helmsman's hand
and paced again our midnight watch
to morning crow!

Then only will I let you go.

∼ ∼ ∼

If I would have you now at peace
I would to a pavane slow every dance
and to the night free every song —
turn every light to fire-glow
on your bed apart
and close my eyes to weep.

Then only will you sleep.

SUPPERTIME: NURSING HOME

My bottom burns with shame
upon its rubber seat.
My ribs congeal in high chair arms.
Bib-ties noose around my neck.
I mumble mashed potatoes on my tongue
and let a snake of custard navigate my throat.
Then one hundred times before they leave me
in my guard-railed bed,
I scrawl on schoolroom slate the evening's date.

What have I so heinous done
to merit this inhuman fate?

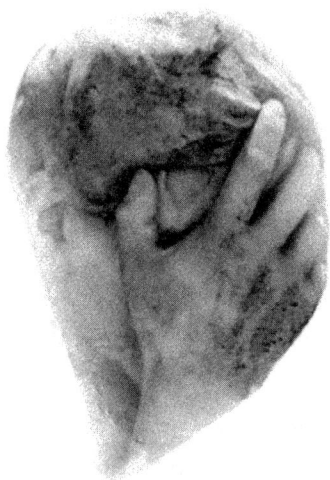

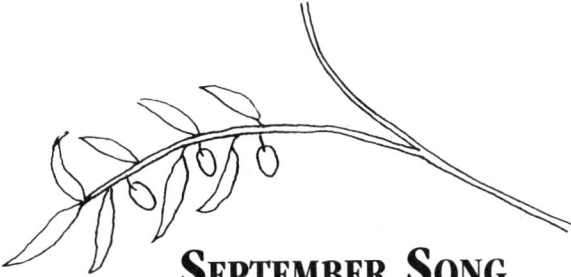

SEPTEMBER SONG

Now is your birth month come again
With soft-scented seeding days
When corn-silk browns and green blades rust
And petals wrinkle from their core
To snare a sated bee once more.

Now tolls the bell one hundred years
In hornpipe we last summer wrote
To dance you to galactic dust
Where, eager, I will follow soon
From my bereft and raging June.

THREE GRACES

NARCISSA

At my cusp of time
with ego ripe as purple fig
I kneel beside the pool to see
reflected ultimate of me.

LYUDMILA

Askew above piano, pressed in glass,
a web of weed entangles sun
and chickory in skeins of wheat.

When she plays Schumann in the Brooklyn flat,
the dried lace trembles in its trap.

MOLLY

Molly at ninety-three required
no litany to be inspired
by memory of Gibraltar days
enjoyed acquiring humid ways;
no Dublin fantasy to speed
her back to Poldy's fetid need.

But Molly now at ninety-four
has all forgotten of before.

NATIVITY

Let April in!
She may at first offend with ragged snow
And ice-chards in her wind-snarled hair.
But in her greed for sun,
her thirst for rivulets that thrum like cellos
under mating bird-flute calls,
she cannot long be either cold or cruel.
For she is pregnant with the Spring
and will be beautiful at birthing.
                              Let April in.

                    2000

GOLBAL WARNING

Let April in again!
She bloomed last year a maiden fair
With apple blossoms in her hair
But now — from far Pacific shores —
She rides *El Niño* to our doors.
Banging shutters, spitting showers,
Scampering goatish on first flowers,
Bending pines to bullying breezes,
Bestrewing wintry coughs and sneezes.
This wanton ragamuffin gypsy
Teases north to old Poughkeepsie,
Where she serves vanilla snows
With Russian sleet before she goes
Across the Catskills and away —
Bequeathing us a gorgeous May.

2001

AFFINITY

Three hundred years away,
three thousand miles apart,
I feel the weight of bending head
with lace-capped eyes intent
upon the paring hand,
while naked I beneath a naked bulb
contort upon an institution bed to reach
with clipper scimitars
my knotted toes.

TO A YOUNG MAN

Like a waiter shuffling on his calloused soles,
Reeking of boredom and old *soupes de jour* —
Fumbling his cache of tips in pocket creases —
Mumbling an abacus of leaden years —
He interminably approaches.

Do not, I beg, until he can compose his face,
Humiliate him with your filial embrace.

A JAPANESE PRINT
TO FRANCES GAAR

Beyond the cherry tree and gardened terrace
ladies move in walkers toward the water
falling pool to pool
and gentlemen with dignity of cane
stroll to the teahouse where up-curling eaves
re-echo samisen and flute in gossip
at the Lady Murasaki's court —

THE ROOKIE

Dark coat, his Brooks shirt buttoned chin to tail,
The bowtie butterflied, grey slacks in pleat,
He greets with grace the diners' muted hail
Then sits, first time in his new home, to eat.

His designated table-mate slow motion
Comes, pulsing Paxil charm from every pore,
Urged forward by strong smell of Bengué lotion,
Her dentures ready bared to bite and bore.

With dignity he pushes back his chair.
With *politesse* he welcomes her, upright.
With poise he bows and seats his lady fair,
Occasioning her grin of rare delight.

"Alzheimer's!" surfs the shoreline of the room.
But he, awash in jetsam, neither hears
Nor sees the mounting flotsam waves of gloom
Until — *Bon-soiring* us — he disappears.

"Goodnight," we whisper from our common fears.

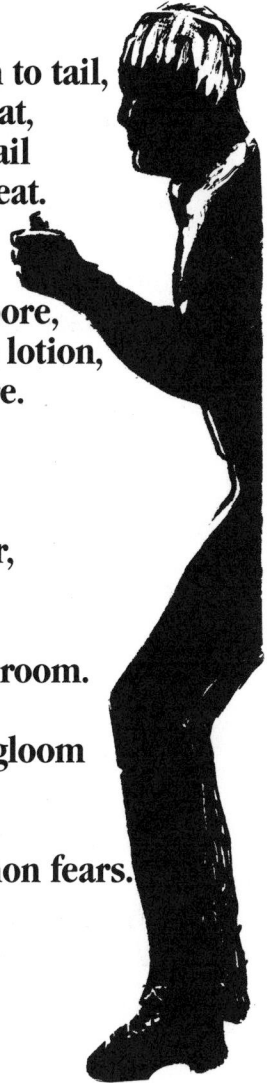

SPRING 2003

When lilacs last in their dooryard bloomed
her son stood at her side to place
a mound of purple on his brother's grave
as bugle mourned.

And when he turned his bright head to depart
she raised his father's gun
from pocket of her skirt
and shot him through the heart.

Tutti Per Tutti

For

Livia

GUYED LINES

Pride goeth before a fall
and haughty blood pressure before a stroke

A stitch in time saves indecent exposure

Send not to ask for whom the bell tolls:
it is a false alarm

An apple a day cuts the doctor's pay

A rolling stone ends up in your kidney

He who hesitates goes hungry

The early bird gets the germ

Love thy neighbor if thou canst

Haste makes the emergency roo

Into each life a little pain must fall

Quoth the maven, "Give us more!"

Love's Labour's Lost on us

Don't put the cart before the hearse

A bird in hand should be tossed in the bush

Water over the dam will extinguish fire
from the bridges you burned behind you

Make Hey! Hey! while you Can-Can

A dollar saved is a dollar spurned

A tisket, a tasket, we don't want a casket yet

Watched pot never grows

Don't sit under the MRI with anyone else but me

Any port in a storm tastes good

Toupée or not toupée — that is the question

Our ten o' clock scholar plays Brahms, Bach and Mahler

Sweet sixty-six and never been hissed

A word from the wise is a surprise

Don't put all your pills in one swallow

Search and ye shall find all those things ye lost yesterday

Do not go gentle into that dark night
for you will be locked out

OLD PRO

I hate to spoil your juvenile illusions
But going on the road is far from fun,
For in the sticks the natives don't respect you,
So here's some hints from one whose tour is done:

You better watch your step in old Chautauqua,
And on the wharf in O'Neill's Provincetown
Where every native is a seasoned critic
Who gladly whets his knife to cut you down.

If once when in Paducah you get raves
And then the next time booked there critics boo,
You must recall the words of H.L. Mencken:
"Tis not the play that stinks it's always you."

Be careful when you play in wasp Nantucket
Where Blacks and Jews are not quite *comme il faut*
And if you're starred as *Shylock* or *Othello*
The whaler lads might boil you in hot *eau.*

I liked to play the one-horse town Niagara
Where nubile girlies liked to play with me.
I would have had no need to buy Viagra
Because my youthful vigor did it free.

The cheapest rooms and sweetest food I know
Were in the boarding houses by the tracks.
Why, just between Atlanta and Valdosta
You'd find the world's best coffee and flapjacks!

When rains pour down in Baltimore, it's steamy,
And snow in Buffalo can close your show.
The sun in Corpus Christi is plain blist'ry
And those Missoula winds can really blow.

Don't seek to have your way with farmers' daughters
Or with those husky sons of prairie grasses.
It's risky to be frisky in Sandusky
Where hicks don't know their elbows from molasses.

In Kalamazoo, Muskogee and Altoona
You may be going over very big.
But count the pay you get from those three houses —
Each manager will cheat you like a pig.

Don't loiter in the lobby in Beloit or
Try to make a date in Kankakee.
And should you get the pox down in Biloxi,
Consult a certain doxy by the sea.

And when you're finally back in dear old Philly
You'll be as thrilled as if you'd reached the Pole,
For every broad on Broad Street is a dilly
And Bookbinder's serves the food that soothes your soul.

Yet nothing can or will beat old New York,
That one and only gritty Great White Way,
Where after boondock tours of trial and labor
An actor hopes to win a starring day.

MARTHA SHERMAN'S HINTS FOR RESIDENTS

Always carry a doggy bag
in case you are served
anything edible.

Avoid eye contact if you wish
to be alone.

Turn down the volume on your
hearing aid when entering the
dining room.

Never snore in the library:
it sets a common tone.

A few drops of vinegar in your
morning glass of water makes
a fine self-starter.

Do not visit another resident's
room unless invited.

It is a smart idea to learn some
Spanish in order to communicate
courteously with staff members.

Never get sick on a weekend.

Walking indoors as well as out is a
preferred activity, but do follow
priorities in hallways: wheelchair,
walker, cane, optimist.

Be polite to your table-mate
so long as he/she does not
eat with his/her knife.

Beware of asking a casual
friend a casual "How are you?"

Be certain to aim your cough
or sneeze in the desired direction.

Avoid using your Christmas gift
cologne on the same occasions
all others do.

It is suggested that if one
anticipates a dinner with beef, pork,
veal, ham, lamb, or chicken, one
generously applies Poligrip —
to the dentures, of course.

Those who are tone-deaf
should firmly excuse themselves
from sing-alongs.

A good listener is priceless
at any age, but no one wants
to hear the details.

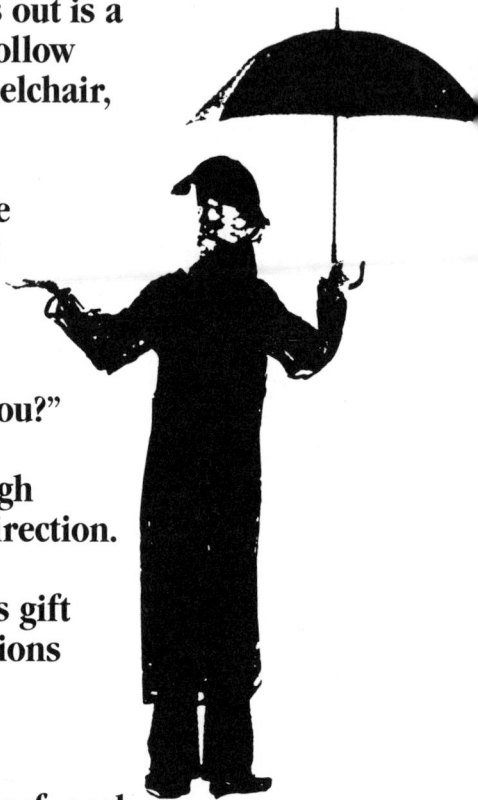

Never sit in a front row when
attending amateur entertainments:
escape in response to physical,
mental, or artistic demand can
be embarrassingly obvious.

Toothpaste applied by brush restores
sparkle to one's jewels, if you
have any after paying your rent.

It is recommended that you
contrive to be the last to
enter lounge or dining room when
you're wearing a new frock or
blazer for the first time.

Good posture is as valuable to
spirits as to health. Martha therefore
proposes that – by whatever means –
residents move through the
years with heads and spirits high.

ALICE IN BLUNDERLAND

I do not remember however I came here.
I do not remember why things are so strange here.
For this is the land of never-no-never
Where mutton is lamb and veal is whatever.
Where chicken flies at me on buffalo wings
And pasta is made of some curious things.
Where nobody wishes to eat the knishes
Made by new Buddhists or other *goyisches*,
Nor order baked ham that is pure Spam what am,
Nor try the roast beef cut from mountain goat ram.
Where only the maddest of cows would confess
That hers was the Swiss steak no one could digest,
And gefilte fish without a dress of horseradish
Is a naked dish shamed into cuisine for Kaddish.

If fate here would hold me, then I'll steal a tin bucket
And one darkest night I will row to Nantucket
Where I will find feathers to pin on a barrel
And fly myself back to my dear Lewis Carroll

PUNNY DEFINITIONS

Agriculture:	A Greek civilization
Aquapuncture:	Watery blow-out
Approximate:	A stand-in spouse
Average:	Declare how old you are
Ballerina:	A game field
Barbeque:	Line up for a haircut
Bargain:	Drink profit
Believe:	Stinger begone!
Bison:	Farewell, junior
Bulbous:	Tulip transportation
Category:	Bloody feline
Chinchilla:	Air conditioning for the face
Contemplate:	With a pattern
Declare:	Fraternity den
Dictator:	Penis spud
Dogma:	A bitch
Exactly:	Precise wind location
Impotent:	Powerful sprite
Infer:	Be-minked
Intense:	Under canvas
Irony:	Strong joint
Irrigate:	A ghostly entranceway

Marginalize:	Distant friends
Misappropriate:	Suitable young lady
Notwithstanding:	Can't be done erect
Oxymoron:	A stupid bullock
Palisades:	Castle workers
Paprika:	Dad smells bad
Paranoia:	Couple bothers you
Parsimony:	Persian currency
Pastime:	Too late
Penal code:	Prison rhinitis
Pilgrim:	Disagreeable medication
Politics:	Parrot parasites
Postpone:	After Johnnycake
Potentate:	Strong number
Prehensile:	Gretl first
Presuppose:	Minister's stockings
Primate:	First Lady
Salutary:	'Allo, 'enry!
Surfboard:	Weary of the waves
Tranquilize:	Peaceful orbs
Willful:	Bill ate too much

CULTURE IN THE GOLDEN YEARS

Do not consider us as snobs
Above amusements of the mobs.
Nor crude nor dude nor prudes nor lewd
If these are now what we conclude:

When *La Bohème* is set to rock
What can a lady do but mock
If Mimi's loud-miked yowls and screeches
Rip to rags Rudolfo's breeches?

I would if I could hang a very large Goya
On the very best wall of a very large foyer,
Picasso on one side, Vermeer on the other,
And serenade all by guitarist Montoya.

O'Casey is my favorite rogue
Of all whom Lady Gregory raised
From poverty of bog and brogue
To be by Broadway critics praised.

I never studied acting with the Strasbergs,
And often felt regret that I had not —
Yet I'd have been true errant fool and knave,
If once embraced by either Lee or wife,
To think that I could ever so behave
As to obey their least demands for life.

A rose is a rose is a rose to Gert Stein,
But her views on botany cannot be mine
For tho' its perfume pleases wher'er it blows
A rose gives *this* sniffer a red, runny nose.

The chickens of one Marcel Proust
Come very slowly home to roost
Since e'en before their flight begin
Monsieur must eat a *madeleine.*

Let me sing like a birdie with Verdi
And float on Debussy's dark wave,
Get drunk with my Mozart, then, flirty,
Waltz off with Dick Strauss to my grave.

A book of Poe's brings wondrous lore
With lovely goose pimples and fears
As well as stuff to make you snore
Thro all your coming tell-tale years.

The *Swan of Tuonela's* no favorite of mine
With his Nordic honking through melodic line.
I muchly prefer Lohengrin's noble bird
[Altho' I confess its bi-species is weird.]

If I could but play the perfection of oboe
(Which no one, 'tis said, can blow good),
With my *L'aprés Midi* every listener would then know
The heavenly sound of high wood.

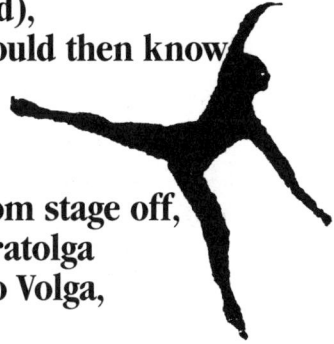

A marvelous dancer was Vasilitamov
Who jetéed and chasséed his rivals from stage off,
'Til one night in rapture he tossed Paratolga
Straight up into air, straight down into Volga,
And that was finale for Vasilitamov.

I'm sad to admit I could never read Beckett,
Hard as I knew I should try.
But to see those two bums sit on stage just awaiting
Always brought tears to my eye.

Oh, I have sown many Wilde oats, my dears,
And gathered all rosebuds I could.
I drank with my eyes (to my greatest surprise)
When lacking the wine that I should.
I even asked Bobby to come be my love
Before our acquaintance grew auld —
But he preferred games with our bonnie Prince Charlie
And I was left out in the cauld.

BRAVA! BRAVO!
(apologies to Irving Berlin)

There's no old ones like stage old ones
Shout "Brava!" and "Bravo!"
Ask him for a buck and he will give it
Ask her for a smile and there you are
They can teach you drama, dance, and daring
For every one is a guiding star
There's no people like show people
To laugh when they are blue
On the day they realize their teeth are gone
They don't let that stop their song
They just put the new ones in where they belong
And go on with their show,
Gotta go on with their show

Yes there's no people like pro people
Of all people you know
Sometimes they are prickly and complaining
Sometimes vain and stubborn as an oak
But who else can give you that good feeling
That you've been talking to glamorous folk?
There's no pros quite like old pros
They never give in
He may not have noticed that his fly's unzipped
He needs a shave, his collar's ripped,
If you tell him he'll just curse a word that's blipped
And go on with his show
Right on with his own show!

Stage oldsters are bold oldsters
Very rare oldies to know.
She may not remember what the day is
And forget it soon as she is told
But when you need nugget of sound wisdom
She is a mine of purest gold
For there's no people like show people
To share what they have learned
He may be as feisty as a fighting cock
She a witch with no warlock
But they'll steer their boat right to that heavenly dock
And open their new show
"Brava and Bravo"!